Dear Parent:

P9-CDV-904

Your child's love of reading starts here!

Every child learns to read in a different way and at his or her own speed. Some go back and forth between reading levels and read favorite books again and again. Others read through each level in order. You can help your young reader improve and become more confident by encouraging his or her own interests and abilities. From books your child reads with you to the first books he or she reads alone, there are I Can Read Books for every stage of reading:

SHARED READING
Basic language, word repetition, and whimsical illustrations, ideal for sharing with your emergent reader

BEGINNING READING
Short sentences, familiar words, and simple concepts for children eager to read on their own

READING WITH HELP
Engaging stories, longer sentences, and language play for developing readers

READING ALONE
Complex plots, challenging vocabulary, and high-interest topics for the independent reader

I Can Read Books have introduced children to the joy of reading since 1957. Featuring award-winning authors and illustrators and a fabulous cast of beloved characters, I Can Read Books set the standard for beginning readers.

A lifetime of discovery begins with the magical words **"I Can Read!"**

Visit www.icanread.com for information
on enriching your child's reading experience.

*For my optical engineer
big brother, David
—L.D.*

*To my favorite engineer
—C.E.*

I Can Read® and I Can Read Book® are trademarks of HarperCollins Publishers.

I Want to Be an Engineer
Copyright © 2021 by HarperCollins Publishers
All rights reserved. Printed in the United States of America.
No part of this book may be used or reproduced in any manner whatsoever without written permission except
in the case of brief quotations embodied in critical articles and reviews. For information address HarperCollins
Children's Books, a division of HarperCollins Publishers, 195 Broadway, New York, NY 10007.
www.icanread.com

ISBN 978-0-06-298958-1 (trade bdg.) — ISBN 978-0-06-298957-4 (pbk.)

Book design by Jeanne Hogle

23 24 25 CWM 10 9 8 7 6 5   ❖   First Edition

1 BEGINNING READING

I Can Read!

I Want to Be an
Engineer

by Laura Driscoll
pictures by Catalina Echeverri

HARPER

An Imprint of HarperCollinsPublishers

My big brother, Joe,

is going to a new school.

"Not just any school!" Joe says.

"An *engineering* school."

I am not sure what that is.

But it looks like engineering

means lots of Joe's favorite things:

space and rockets.

When Joe grows up,

he wants to build rockets.

"It is called *aerospace engineering*,"

Joe says.

The principal gives us a tour.

She asks me,

"Maybe someday

you will come here, too?"

I shake my head.

"I do not like space," I say.

"I like robots!"

I show her my robot dog.

"Engineering is not all about space,"
the principal says.

"Engineers are problem solvers."

"They use science

to plan and build things.

There are all kinds of engineers."

"I am an engineer," Mom says

on the way home.

Huh?

I thought Mom was an architect.

"I am an *architectural engineer*,"

Mom says.

"I make plans for buildings.

They have to look nice.

They have to be buildable.

And they can't cost too much to build.

It is a puzzle!"

The next day,

Mom takes me to work with her.

There are so many workers!

They are building a building

that Mom designed.

"There are lots of engineers here,"
Mom says.

We meet an engineer

when we check in at the office.

"I make sure the building

is built strong and safe," he says.

"From the concrete at the bottom
to the roof on top."
He is a *structural engineer*.

Down in the basement,
workers put in pipes.
"Some pipes bring water in,"
this engineer says.

"Others carry wastewater out.

They run all through the building."

She is a *plumbing engineer*.

Upstairs, workers put in
wires and cables.

Some will carry electricity
to lights, fire alarms, and more.
The *electrical engineer* decides
where they all go.

Some cables are for phone lines
and computers.

How many does this floor need?

The *network engineer* will decide.

Outside, an engineer takes notes.

Which way

should the solar panels face?

How can the building be

more Earth-friendly?

He is an *environmental engineer*.

Another engineer just got here.

He is going to work on

the elevator.

This engineer is an expert

on how machines work.

He is a *mechanical engineer.*

"Want to meet my helper?"

asks the mechanical engineer.

"My helper climbs up the elevator shaft.

It drills holes in the concrete.

And it does it all by itself!"

"It is a robot!" I shout.

Mom says,

"Guess who designed that robot."

29

"An engineer?" I ask.

Mom nods.

"A *robotic engineer*," she says.

Just think!

I could make robots.

I want to be an engineer!

Meet the Engineers

Aerospace engineer
An engineer who designs planes or spacecraft

Architectural engineer
An engineer who draws up plans for buildings

Structural engineer
An engineer who makes sure a structure is built to be strong and safe

Plumbing engineer
An engineer who plans a system of pipes that carry water or gas

Electrical engineer
An engineer who makes, tests, or fixes things that carry electricity

Network engineer
An engineer who plans and sets up connections between computers

Environmental engineer
An engineer who finds ways to build that are gentle on nature

Mechanical engineer
An engineer who is an expert on machines and how they work

Robotic engineer
An engineer who designs, builds, or fixes robots